THE
GOSPEL
ACCORDING TO
THOMAS

An Interpretation

From someone
who has loved Jesus
from an early age

CAMERON McCOLL

Acknowledgments

I have referenced some teachings and sayings of Ramana Maharshi, Da Free John, Francis Lucille, Robert Adams, and others. My intention throughout has simply been to express what comes to me, as lucidly and succinctly as possible, using whoever's words or teachings appear to resonate in the context.

Background

Growing up in Edinburgh, Scotland, before the internet, or email, and with few books to be found on the bigger questions of life, as a young teenager I turned to the only book available to me to address my questions—The King James Bible. Hungry for truth I sifted through its pages, and I found sustenance.

Mentally highlighting all the new testament passages which spoke to me, I became aware of the presence of the Holy Spirit in my life.

Many years later, when introduced to the Gospel According to Thomas, imagine my surprise when I saw all these highlighted passages captured in one book.

I felt moved to recreate the words that had been written all those years ago.

INTRODUCTION

Peasants digging at the base of a cliff along the Nile River, in 1945, unearthed a tall, sealed clay jar that had been secreted beneath a boulder. The site of the discovery near the village of Nag Hammadi in Upper Egypt, about 200 miles south of Cairo is three miles from what had been the ancient Christian monastery of St. Pachomius, founded in the 4th Century.

The jar, when broken open, held thirteen leather-bound volumes, or codices, which contained 52 tractates, now collectively known as the Nag Hammadi Library. The Gospel According To Thomas was one of these.

The writing on the papyrus tractates was in Coptic, an ancient Egyptian language (still used in rituals of the Coptic Church in Egypt and Ethiopia).

In 1978, the first complete English translation was published as *The Nag Hammadi Library*, edited by James Robinson of Claremont Graduate School.

A subsequent translation by Thomas Lambdin has been used as the source text below.

Scholars now largely agree that the Gospel According To Thomas was written concurrently with the other New Testament gospels, or possibly even earlier. Its unadorned structure suggests it may even represent a more original document than the other New Testament Gospels. It is interesting to note that It has no chronological narrative;

no biographical detail, such as a birth scene; no account of a ritual with John the Baptist. There are no miracles; no crowds of followers; no temple confrontations. No crucifixion or resurrection tales; no theology of sin, judgment, hell or redemption. No misogyny (Salome and Mary are two of the five disciples named); no discussion of founding a church; no talk of a Second Coming; and no rephrasing of Old Testament commandments.

THE GOSPEL
ACCORDING TO THOMAS,
with Interpretations

These are the secret sayings which the living Jesus
spoke and which Didymos Judas Thomas wrote down.

— 1 —

And he said, "Whoever finds the interpretation of these sayings will not experience death."

When you truly understand what I am saying to you, you will know that death is an illusion. The body dies but you do not die, for you were never born. That which was never born can never die, and that which is born, was never truly alive.

— 2 —

Jesus said, "Let him who seeks continue seeking until he finds. When he finds, he will become troubled. When he becomes troubled, he will be astonished, and he will rule over the All."

We have to be diligent in our search for truth. Once we have a glimpse of our true nature we may become troubled because we come to see that our entire view of ourselves and the world is false—we are living in a house built on sand. When the full implications are absorbed, we become amazed, and having arrived at a new understanding of ourselves and the world, we realise that all is well and everything is unfolding as it should.

— 3 —

Jesus said, "If those who lead you say to you, 'See, the kingdom is in the sky,' then the birds of the sky will precede you. If they say to you, 'It is in the sea,' then the fish will precede you. Rather, the kingdom is inside of you, and it is outside of you. When you come to know yourselves, then you will become known, and you will realize that it is you who are the sons of the living father. But if you will not know yourselves, you dwell in poverty and it is you who are that poverty."

The kingdom which we seek is not of this world, therefore the world's creatures cannot lead us to it. This world, indeed the entire universe, is cradled within the reality which we seek, which in itself is formless. It is nowhere and everywhere—inside us and outside us. It is not other than us. It is our true reality. We have the choice to know who we truly are or to remain in ignorance, believing ourselves to be these feeble 'shacks' which are born, live and die.

— 4 —

Jesus said, "The man old in days will not hesitate to ask a small child seven days old about the place of life, and he will live. For many who are first will become last, and they will become one and the same."

When we become wise and undress ourselves, and when we are open, and slough off the false layers of identity accumulated over a lifetime, then through grace, we are shown our true identity. We become humble, and open to seeing the truth wherever it may be found. Those who in ignorance believe themselves to be body-minds, whether they be leaders or followers in the world, shall achieve equality in death.

— 5 —

Jesus said, "Recognize what is in your sight, and that which is hidden from you will become plain to you. For there is nothing hidden which will not become manifest."

When we are able to truly recognise the objects in front of us, we are also able to recognise ourselves, for we are not objects. When any object is seen for what it truly is, then all objects, subtle or gross, indeed the entire universe and everything in it, are also seen. Their reality is seen, which is consciousness itself.

— 6 —

His disciples questioned him and said to him, "Do you want us to fast? How shall we pray? Shall we give alms? What diet shall we observe?"

Jesus said, "Do not tell lies, and do not do what you hate, for all things are plain in the sight of heaven. For nothing hidden will not become manifest, and nothing covered will remain without being uncovered."

The disciples ask Jesus, "How shall we live in the world?"

Jesus says "It's not your activities that matter, but your integrity. If you want to find the truth, then live openly, truthfully, knowing that all is seen, and follow happiness".

— 7 —

Jesus said, "Blessed is the lion which becomes man when consumed by man; and cursed is the man whom the lion consumes, and the lion becomes man."

The world is the lion, maya. When truly seen, it is understood to be consciousness itself. When not seen, it becomes man's reality and he is destined to a life of suffering.

— 8 —

And he said, "The man is like a wise fisherman who cast his net into the sea and drew it up from the sea full of small fish. Among them the wise fisherman found a fine large fish. He threw all the small fish back into the sea and chose the large fish without difficulty. Whoever has ears to hear, let him hear."

There are many pretty flowers on the path up to the sacred temple. He who is single minded in his desire for truth ignores them and keeps walking directly towards his heart's desire on the temple altar.

9

Jesus said, "Now the sower went out, took a handful (of seeds), and scattered them. Some fell on the road; the birds came and gathered them up. Others fell on the rock, did not take root in the soil, and did not produce ears. And others fell on thorns; they choked the seed(s) and worms ate them. And others fell on the good soil and it produced good fruit: it bore sixty per measure and a hundred and twenty per measure."

Some stones grow warm when drawn close to the fire, but quickly cool when taken away. A very few who wish to know their true identity, are like dry sticks, ready to be burned to ash in the fire of understanding. Those few shine brightly in the world. Their influence spreads far and wide.

— 10 —

Jesus said, "I have cast fire upon the world, and see, I am guarding it until it blazes."

The truth is revolutionary. It shatters all our pre-existing notions of 'reality'. It undermines all societies power structures. Jesus knew exactly what he was doing—he lit the touch-paper of a firestorm of change.

— 11 —

Jesus said, "This heaven will pass away, and the one above it will pass away. The dead are not alive, and the living will not die. In the days when you consumed what is dead, you made it what is alive. When you come to dwell in the light, what will you do? On the day when you were one you became two. But when you become two, what will you do?"

Everything that has a beginning has an end. If you seek that which is eternal, you must look for that which is without beginning. Those who are in ignorance, dead to the truth, know death. Those who are awake to truth recognise that they are life itself, eternal. For them death does not exist. In ignorance you took the world, materiality, to be the ultimate reality. Now that you see the truth, what will you do? Once you were whole, oneness itself, but you chose to experience separation. Now that you experience life as a fragment, what will you do?

— 12 —

The disciples said to Jesus, "We know that you will depart from us. Who is to be our leader?"

Jesus said to them, "Wherever you are, you are to go to James the righteous, for whose sake heaven and earth came into being."

No commentary.

—— 13 ——

Jesus said to his disciples, "Compare me to someone and tell me whom I am like."

Simon Peter said to him, "You are like a righteous angel."

Matthew said to him, "You are like a wise philosopher."

Thomas said to him, "Master, my mouth is wholly incapable of saying whom you are like."

Jesus said, "I am not your master. Because you have drunk, you have become intoxicated from the bubbling spring which I have measured out."

And he took him and withdrew and told him three things. When Thomas returned to his companions, they asked him, "What did Jesus say to you?"

Thomas said to them, "If I tell you one of the things which he told me, you will pick up stones and throw them at me; a fire will come out of the stones and burn you up."

Jesus tested the disciples understanding. Thomas alone understood Jesus' true nature. Jesus told Thomas that because he had been open to the truth, and had come to realise it for himself, Jesus was no longer his master. In other words, they had become equals in truth.

— 14 —

Jesus said to them, "If you fast, you will give rise to sin for yourselves; and if you pray, you will be condemned; and if you give alms, you will do harm to your spirits. When you go into any land and walk about in the districts, if they receive you, eat what they will set before you, and heal the sick among them. For what goes into your mouth will not defile you, but that which issues from your mouth—it is that which will defile you."

Jesus told his disciples "The Truth is not to be found outside of you in the world. Doing good deeds is not truth if it comes from a sense of personal doer-ship". The rules about what you should, or should not eat, do not matter. It's what comes out of your mouth which matters, for your words can be spoken in truth or in ignorance.

— 15 —

Jesus said, "When you see one who was not born of woman, prostrate yourselves on your faces and worship him. That one is your father."

Jesus said, "When you encounter someone who recognizes their own eternity, aware of who they truly are, never having been born, and never to die, prostrate yourselves before them, because this one is your true parent, capable of guiding you home".

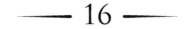

Jesus said, "Men think, perhaps, that it is peace which I have come to cast upon the world. They do not know that it is dissension which I have come to cast upon the earth: fire, sword, and war. For there will be five in a house: three will be against two, and two against three, the father against the son, and the son against the father. And they will stand solitary."

Jesus mission was to tell the truth about what is real, and who we are. It is a polar opposite view to the conventional one, and undermines it entirely. Those who come to understand the true nature of reality cannot fail but to put it first. All worldly relationship structures are superceded, and become redundant, when seen in the light of greater clarity. A secret, once learned, cannot be unlearned.

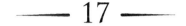

— 17 —

Jesus said, "I shall give you what no eye has seen and what no ear has heard and what no hand has touched and what has never occurred to the human mind."

Jesus came to show us what was hidden in plain sight, in front of us all the time. So close we couldn't see it, yet right there always. Like the face hidden in a child's puzzle drawing, until we see it, it's not there, however once seen, it cannot again become hidden.

—— 18 ——

The disciples said to Jesus, "Tell us how our end will be."

Jesus said, "Have you discovered, then, the beginning, that you look for the end? For where the beginning is, there will the end be. Blessed is he who will take his place in the beginning; he will know the end and will not experience death."

Identified with their mortal human bodies, the disciples asked Jesus what fate awaited them.

Jesus asks them, "Do you remember the beginning of consciousness? Your body had a beginning, but did you? In order for something to end, it has to begin. Look for your beginning. When you come to see that there never was one, you will also come to understand that there can be no end, and that death is an illusion". Time itself takes its reality from consciousness, from God.

19

Jesus said, "Blessed is he who came into being before he came into being. If you become my disciples and listen to my words, these stones will minister to you. For there are five trees for you in Paradise which remain undisturbed summer and winter and whose leaves do not fall. Whoever becomes acquainted with them will not experience death."

The one who came into being, before he came into being, is the creator himself, that which is prior to all creation, and the source of all creation. Every object in creation has the power to reveal its source—even inanimate objects such as stones have this power, for the one who has eyes to truly look.

— 20 —

The disciples said to Jesus, "Tell us what the kingdom of heaven is like."

He said to them, "It is like a mustard seed. It is the smallest of all seeds. But when it falls on tilled soil, it produces a great plant and becomes a shelter for birds of the sky."

Initially awareness, consciousness is taken for granted. It's just there—of no great significance. However when we look deeply we see that it is the support of everything, and when we look deeper still we see that in fact there is nothing truly real, other than awareness, consciousness itself.

— 21 —

Mary said to Jesus, "Whom are your disciples like?"

He said, "They are like children who have settled in a field which is not theirs. When the owners of the field come, they will say, 'Let us have back our field.' They (will) undress in their presence in order to let them have back their field and to give it back to them.

Truly we are not of this world, rather the world is in us. When the world tries to claim us back we shed all identity with it and return to our true nature.

Therefore I say, if the owner of a house knows that the thief is coming, he will begin his vigil before he comes and will not let him dig through into his house of his domain to carry away his goods. You, then, be on your guard against the world. Arm yourselves with great strength lest the robbers find a way to come to you, for the difficulty which you expect will (surely) materialize. Let there be among you a man of understanding. When the grain ripened, he came quickly with his sickle in his hand and reaped it. Whoever has ears to hear, let him hear."

Identity with the body-mind claims us almost unawares. It is the present orientation of this world. We have to be awake to the ways we identify with the body-mind, both gross and subtle, in order not to slip into unconsciousness, into separation and suffering.

—— 22 ——

Jesus saw infants being suckled. He said to his disciples, "These infants being suckled are like those who enter the kingdom."

They said to him, "Shall we then, as children, enter the kingdom?"

Jesus said to them, "When you make the two one, and when you make the inside like the outside and the outside like the inside, and the above like the below, and when you make the male and the female one and the same, so that the male not be male nor the female female; and when you fashion eyes in the place of an eye, and a hand in place of a hand, and a foot in place of a foot, and a likeness in place of a likeness; then will you enter the kingdom."

Prior to the birth of ego, with no sense of separation—this is the babe's innocence of which Jesus speaks. Further, he says, when you recover that childlike state, seeing no bodily boundary, no separation between all, when as he says, the outside is the same as the inside and when the underlying oneness of all apparent opposites is seen, then you will have found home, peace, and an end to suffering.

23

Jesus said, "I shall choose you, one out of a thousand, and two out of ten thousand, and they shall stand as a single one."

We think that as humans we choose, but in fact our thoughts just arrive, unbidden. The real chooser is consciousness itself, which Jesus knows himself to be. It appears that consciousness only expresses a strong desire for truth through a few body-minds. These individuals, recognising their true nature, understand that they are not other than consciousness itself.

24

His disciples said to him, "Show us the place where you are, since it is necessary for us to seek it."

He said to them, "Whoever has ears, let him hear. There is light within a man of light, and he lights up the whole world. If he does not shine, he is darkness."

The disciples ask, "Where is this place of truth where you stand?" When Jesus says to them, "Whoever has ears, let him hear", he means, "Abandon your beliefs and preconceived ideas and be open to the possibility that what I am telling you is true." Then in answer to their question he tells them, "There is light within a man of light." In other words his instruction is to follow the light to find the truth they seek. For light we could also say, bliss, or happiness. So the instruction is to follow light, bliss, or happiness to find truth.

— 25 —

Jesus said, "Love your brother like your soul, guard him like the pupil of your eye."

Our brothers and sisters and we, are one. To love one another is to live in this oneness.

— 26 —

Jesus said, "You see the mote in your brother's eye, but you do not see the beam in your own eye. When you cast the beam out of your own eye, then you will see clearly to cast the mote from your brother's eye."

We see other peoples prejudices, beliefs and conditioned responses, but fail to see our own. Through investigation of our own thought patterns and unexamined beliefs, we arrive at a clarity of mind. Only then can we help our friends with their investigation.

—— **27** ——

\<Jesus said,\> "If you do not fast as regards the world, you will not find the kingdom. If you do not observe the Sabbath as a Sabbath, you will not see the father."

If we come to understand that the pursuit of worldly desires does not lead to the lasting happiness we seek, then we need to become wise and act upon that understanding, by giving up our addiction to worldly pleasures. This action provides us with the opportunity to, 'Observe the Sabbath', in other words, to devote time and energy to that which matters to us the most.

Jesus said, "I took my place in the midst of the world, and I appeared to them in flesh. I found all of them intoxicated; I found none of them thirsty. And my soul became afflicted for the sons of men, because they are blind in their hearts and do not have sight; for empty they came into the world, and empty too they seek to leave the world. But for the moment they are intoxicated. When they shake off their wine, then they will repent."

Jesus found people fully engaged in the dream of worldly existence, driven by fears and desires, living blindly, without even the recognition of their true heart's desire. He saw that until they looked beyond the world of objects for the happiness they sought, they would be destined to a life of separation and suffering. Still, he held out the hope that the day would come, when they would look beyond this apparent reality, and develop a thirst for truth.

— 29 —

Jesus said, "If the flesh came into being because of spirit, it is a wonder. But if spirit came into being because of the body, it is a wonder of wonders. Indeed, I am amazed at how this great wealth has made its home in this poverty."

Consciousness, God, gave rise to the universe and all beings— this in itself is remarkable. What is absurd (a wonder of wonders) is to imagine that this fleshly fragment gave rise to consciousness, God. Indeed Jesus is amazed that consciousness manifests itself in man.

— 30 —

Jesus said, "Where there are three gods, they are gods. Where there are two or one, I am with him."

I suspect a mistranslation, "Where there are three gods, they are gods. Where the two are one, I am with him". The interpretation of the alternative translation would be:

Jesus does not deny the possibility of a multiplicity of deities, however they are of no interest to him. His focus is solely upon the non-dual oneness which underpins all creation.

31

Jesus said, "No prophet is accepted in his own village; no physician heals those who know him."

We may shed identity with our body-minds, but that does not mean that others will cease to identify us as they did before.

—— 32 ——

Jesus said, "A city being built on a high mountain and fortified cannot fall, nor can it be hidden."

The man who has arrived at certainty as to his true nature cannot lose it, nor can this certainty be hidden.

—— **33** ——

Jesus said, "Preach from your housetops that which you will hear in your ear. For no one lights a lamp and puts it under a bushel, nor does he put it in a hidden place, but rather he sets it on a lamp stand so that everyone who enters and leaves will see its light."

Jesus encourages his followers to speak out about what they have come to understand through his teaching. He wants everyone to be able to benefit from this good news. Those who have understood shine, and the light they emanate is there for all to see, and be guided by.

— 34 —

Jesus said, "If a blind man leads a blind man, they will both fall into a pit."

To those who would teach—make sure your motives are pure and your vision clear. To those who seek a teacher—use your intelligence and discrimination to ensure the authenticity of your chosen teacher. Do not settle for less than an inner, "Yes!"

Jesus said, "It is not possible for anyone to enter the house of a strong man and take it by force unless he binds his hands; then he will (be able to) ransack his house."

The world cannot force us into identification with it unless we allow it to. Once identified as individuals, with apparently separate individual consciousness' however, we lose all freedom and are driven solely by our fears and desires.

— 36 —

Jesus said, "Do not be concerned from morning until evening and from evening until morning about what you will wear."

"Do not be identified with outward appearances, for this is not who you are—rather find out your true identity."

— 37 —

His disciples said, "When will you become revealed to us and when shall we see you?"

Jesus said, "When you disrobe without being ashamed and take up your garments and place them under your feet like little children and tread on them, then will you see the son of the living one, and you will not be afraid."

When we no longer identify with our body-minds, nakedness is of no concern, and fear is seen as just another feeling arising, part of the old story of the separate 'me'—another object in our awareness, no longer relevant.

—— 38 ——

Jesus said, "Many times have you desired to hear these words which I am saying to you, and you have no one else to hear them from. There will be days when you will look for me and will not find me."

There is an urgency to Jesus' words. Teachers like Jesus who come into the world are so precious. They are like an oasis in the desert for those who thirst for understanding. It is our responsibility not to squander this gift when it is presented, but to embrace it completely.

— 39 —

Jesus said, "The Pharisees and the scribes have taken the keys of knowledge (gnosis) and hidden them. They themselves have not entered, nor have they allowed to enter those who wish to. You, however, be as wise as serpents and as innocent as doves."

Without the presence of a teacher, words of truth handed down over generations become dogma. The power structures built around the teachings become corrupted, and religions are born. These religions, and their hierarchies, speak the words of truth without understanding their true meaning, moreover with a vested interest in having their meaning not communicated. In this environment, for Jesus' disciples to create a teaching movement which is authentic and successful, they will have to be 'as wise as serpents and as innocent as doves'.

Jesus said, "A grapevine has been planted outside of the father, but being unsound, it will be pulled up by its roots and destroyed."

The 'grapevine planted outside the father' is the pseudo-reality of man, the world of maya. It claims to be outwith the realm and control of the creator. It's false claims will be exposed, and it will cease to be.

— 41 —

Jesus said, "Whoever has something in his hand will receive more, and whoever has nothing will be deprived of even the little he has."

The man who, 'has nothing who will be deprived of even the little he has', thinks he has something. He is the man of the world, who thinks he has control of his thoughts, his body, his actions. This he will discover to be an illusion. The man who, 'has something in his hand who will receive more', has had some glimpse of truth, some measure of understanding . He will be guided to further understanding.

—— 42 ——

Jesus said, "Become passers-by."

Leave this world alone. We are in it, we see it, but we are not of it.

43

His disciples said to him, "Who are you, that you should say these things to us?"

<Jesus said to them,> "You do not realize who I am from what I say to you, but you have become like the Jews, for they (either) love the tree and hate its fruit (or) love the fruit and hate the tree."

The Tree of Life stood in the Garden of Eden, from which Adam and Eve were cast out. It stands for God, truth, love, beauty. The fruit of the tree is creation, the universe and all within it. The disciples held concepts, beliefs and a world view based on Jewish teachings, and challenged Jesus accordingly. Jesus said, 'You don't recognise the truth I speak because of your entrenched beliefs. You either love God to the exclusion of the world, or you love the objects of the world and are blind to God. In truth there is no such duality'.

— 44 —

Jesus said, "Whoever blasphemes against the father will be forgiven, and whoever blasphemes against the son will be forgiven, but whoever blasphemes against the holy spirit will not be forgiven either on earth or in heaven."

In this context, the father and the son are symbols for truth, however the holy spirit refers to our true nature, to what we truly are. To deny one's true nature is to condemn oneself to remain in the false, conditioned view of reality. In other words it is we who through our choice, deny ourselves the opportunity to remember who we truly are, for we are the forgiver.

—— 45 ——

Jesus said, "Grapes are not harvested from thorns, nor are figs gathered from thistles, for they do not produce fruit. A good man brings forth good from his storehouse; an evil man brings forth evil things from his evil storehouse, which is in his heart, and says evil things. For out of the abundance of the heart he brings forth evil things."

Ultimately, there is only love, but within love exists ignorance. From this ignorance spring forth ignorant actions and behaviour. There is no evil outside of God, for nothing is outside of God. Rather, evil is that which arises from ignorance of our true nature. Thus, this is the manner in which, from the abundance of the heart, ignorant actions and behaviour arise.

— 46 —

Jesus said, "Among those born of women, from Adam until John the Baptist, there is no one so superior to John the Baptist that his eyes should not be lowered (before him). Yet I have said, whichever one of you comes to be a child will be acquainted with the kingdom and will become superior to John."

Men may not be created equal, but they are still men. The one who recognises his true nature is superior to all men because he sees beyond the human form, indeed beyond all form, to his true nature which is formless.

— 47 —

Jesus said, "It is impossible for a man to mount two horses or to stretch two bows. And it is impossible for a servant to serve two masters; otherwise, he will honor the one and treat the other contemptuously. No man drinks old wine and immediately desires to drink new wine. And new wine is not put into old wineskins, lest they burst; nor is old wine put into a new wineskin, lest it spoil it. An old patch is not sewn onto a new garment, because a tear would result."

Egoic human existence and entrance into the kingdom of God are mutually incompatible. It is not possible for a man to know his true nature without first exposing the falsity of his belief in a separate individual consciousness. It is like the face hidden in a child's puzzle. Before being seen, to all intents and purposes, it does not exist. Once seen however, it cannot again be lost.

Jesus said, "If two make peace with each other in this one house, they will say to the mountain, 'Move Away,' and it will move away."

Out of nothing more than a series of perceptions we make a world, and call it reality. We give primacy to this world, and secondary reality to the consciousness which gives rise to the perceptions. These perceptions out of which we make a world, are nothing other than consciousness itself, and we are nothing other than that. When this is seen, when these apparently separate aspects of reality are seen as one reality, when the, 'Two make peace with each other in this one house', then the insubstantial nature of the world is also seen, and they can say to the mountain, 'Move Away' and it will move away'.

49

Jesus said, "Blessed are the solitary and elect, for you will find the kingdom. For you are from it, and to it you will return."

Swimming against the tide of humanity requires clear, fearless seeing, an independence of mind and a willingness to travel alone. That which we seek has these same qualities of fearlessness, independence and autonomy, for it stands alone as truth.

Jesus said, "If they say to you, 'Where did you come from?', say to them, 'We came from the light, the place where the light came into being on its own accord and established itself and became manifest through their image.' If they say to you, 'Is it you?', say, 'We are its children, we are the elect of the living father.' If they ask you, 'What is the sign of your father in you?', say to them, 'It is movement and repose.'"

The absolute cannot be described, only pointed towards. Jesus uses metaphors to help his disciples communicate his message to the world, in words that could be understood, remembered, and passed down. His description of the sign of the father in the disciples as being, 'movement and repose', describes the peace and inner stillness ever present in those who know their true nature, even as they live and act in the world.

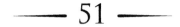

— 51 —

His disciples said to him, "When will the repose of the dead come about, and when will the new world come?"

He said to them, "What you look forward to has already come, but you do not recognize it."

Whatever begins, also ends. If the peace which we seek is truly eternal, then it must always have been present. It's been right here all the time, since the beginning of time. Time itself exists only within this greater reality. Jesus tells his disciples, 'You do not need to wait for anything, rather you need to see what is already the reality of your existence'.

52

His disciples said to him, "Twenty-four prophets spoke in Israel, and all of them spoke in you."

He said to them, "You have omitted the one living in your presence and have spoken (only) of the dead."

A prophet speaks of the future. A true prophet recognises that the future has no independent reality and exists only within consciousness, or God. The truth is alive in this moment. We may inherit valuable teachings from those who have died, but for those who seek to know the truth, there is no substitute for the presence of a living teacher.

53

His disciples said to him, "Is circumcision beneficial or not?"

He said to them, "If it were beneficial, their father would beget them already circumcised from their mother. Rather, the true circumcision in spirit has become completely profitable."

In the Jewish tradition circumcision is used to physically mark the covenant between man and God. It is however a spiritual covenant, not a physical one, that is beneficial, in which we make a spiritual commitment to live as truth.

—— 54 ——

Jesus said, "Blessed are the poor, for yours is the kingdom of heaven."

Every human needs basic necessities to live. Beyond this however, the world of material objects has the ability to hypnotise us. It's an addiction of accumulation, a constant cycle of sense of lack, followed by desire and then short-lived fulfillment. Much of the world lives constantly in this trance, in which our happiness and attention are placed always in the future, out of reach. "Blessed are the poor," Jesus says, for they have the opportunity to live in the present, and know happiness in the simplicity of daily life.

— 55 —

Jesus said, "Whoever does not hate his father and his mother cannot become a disciple to me. And whoever does not hate his brothers and sisters and take up his cross in my way will not be worthy of me."

To identify those around us as father, mother, brother, or sister is to make this world real, to give primacy to this reality, and to identify ourselves with it. We have to look beyond these worldly appearances, to the deeper truth, for only when we know who we truly are, can we know the true nature of others, including those closest to us.

Jesus said, "Whoever has come to understand the world has found (only) a corpse, and whoever has found a corpse is superior to the world."

To understand the world is to recognise that it is made entirely of perceptions, nothing more. From these perceptions we create a concept of 'world'. The world has no independent reality, no life of its own. Without consciousness, which gives rise to the perceptions, there could be no world. Those who have discovered this understand that the world's true reality is consciousness itself, or God.

—— 57 ——

Jesus said, "The kingdom of the father is like a man who had good seed. His enemy came by night and sowed weeds among the good seed. The man did not allow them to pull up the weeds; he said to them, 'I am afraid that you will go intending to pull up the weeds and pull up the wheat along with them.' For on the day of the harvest the weeds will be plainly visible, and they will be pulled up and burned."

The kingdom of the father referred to here represents man's ultimate potential, his journey home. It is not intended to describe all of creation, for nothing exists outside of God.

The enemy is ego, man's adventure in forgetfulness. It is given the time and opportunity to take seed, grow, and flourish. The freedom remains however to see the truth and return home, to the pristine state, for ultimately the one who sows is the one who harvests.

— 58 —

Jesus said, "Blessed is the man who has suffered and found life."

Grace does not hesitate to use any and all circumstances of life, to hold a mirror up to us, to provide the opportunity for us to see things as they really are, to show us the way home. Often it is the most challenging circumstances of life which offer the greatest opportunities to travel home.

59

Jesus said, "Take heed of the living one while you are alive, lest you die and seek to see him and be unable to do so."

The end to suffering and the road to peace, is to know our true nature here and now. This understanding is most efficiently received in the presence of a living teacher.

— 60 —

<They saw> a Samaritan carrying a lamb on his way to Judea. He said to his disciples, "That man is round about the lamb."

They said to him, "So that he may kill it and eat it."

He said to them, "While it is alive, he will not eat it, but only when he has killed it and it has become a corpse."

They said to him, "He cannot do so otherwise."

He said to them, "You too, look for a place for yourself within repose, lest you become a corpse and be eaten."

The body is truly not alive. It has no independent existence. It is a dead thing animated for a time, by life itself. It is life which is real, alive. His admonition to the disciples is to find this life which they are, in the stillness within, now while embodied.

— 61 —

Jesus said, "Two will rest on a bed: the one will die, and the other will live."

Salome said, "Who are you, man, that you ... have come up on my couch and eaten from my table?"

Jesus said to her, "I am he who exists from the undivided. I was given some of the things of my father."

<...> "I am your disciple."

<...> "Therefore I say, if he is destroyed, he will be filled with light, but if he is divided, he will be filled with darkness."

As men and women, we have one freedom only—to choose to remember who we are, or to remain in ignorance. Death is ignorance, for it exists only in ignorance. Each must make their own decision.

Salome asks, 'Who is this person who has become so central in my life?' Jesus responds that, 'He comes from oneness, is not separate from the oneness, and that he reflects some of the many facets of the oneness'.

In destruction there is absorption, resulting in unity, or light. In division there is separation, resulting in duality, and suffering.

—— 62 ——

Jesus said, "It is to those who are worthy of my mysteries that I tell my mysteries. Do not let your left (hand) know what your right (hand) is doing."

Jesus was a political figure in that he used all his faculties, including his intelligence, together with an understanding of the world around him, to communicate his message. He did not challenge the establishment head to head. Rather he taught those who were open to him, thereby almost unnoticed (at least initially), establishing a groundswell of change.

—— 63 ——

Jesus said, "There was a rich man who had much money. He said, 'I shall put my money to use so that I may sow, reap, plant, and fill my storehouse with produce, with the result that I shall lack nothing.' Such were his intentions, but that same night he died. Let him who has ears hear."

We humans have an uncanny ability not to see, what we don't want to see. Death is around the corner for all of us. No amount of effort to secure the future of this body-mind is going to succeed, no matter how much we try. We have to see the folly in this, and look elsewhere for salvation. This is why Jesus says, 'Let him who has ears hear'.

— 64 —

Jesus said, "A man had received visitors. And when he had prepared the dinner, he sent his servant to invite the guests.

He went to the first one and said to him, 'My master invites you.' He said, 'I have claims against some merchants. They are coming to me this evening. I must go and give them my orders. I ask to be excused from the dinner.'

He went to another and said to him, 'My master has invited you.' He said to him, 'I have just bought a house and am required for the day. I shall not have any spare time.'

He went to another and said to him, 'My master invites you.' He said to him, 'My friend is going to get married, and I am to prepare the banquet. I shall not be able to come. I ask to be excused from the dinner.'

He went to another and said to him, 'My master invites you.' He said to him, 'I have just bought a farm, and I am on my way to collect the rent. I shall not be able to come. I ask to be excused.'

The servant returned and said to his master, 'Those whom you invited to the dinner have asked to be excused.' The master said to his servant, 'Go outside to the streets and bring back those whom you happen to meet, so that they may dine.' Businessmen and merchants will not enter the places of my father."

The greater our investment in the world, the more we think we stand to lose by surrendering to a higher power. We deeply believe the world to be real and spend many years shoring up our defences against material lack. Deep inside we know the battle to be unwinnable, yet nonetheless we cling tenaciously to our illusions of independent existence. Such is the human condition. The less invested in the world we are, the more open we become to other possibilities.

— 65 —

He said, "There was a good man who owned a vineyard. He leased it to tenant farmers so that they might work it and he might collect the produce from them. He sent his servant so that the tenants might give him the produce of the vineyard. They seized his servant and beat him, all but killing him. The servant went back and told his master. The master said, 'Perhaps he did not recognize them.' He sent another servant. The tenants beat this one as well. Then the owner sent his son and said, 'Perhaps they will show respect to my son.' Because the tenants knew that it was he who was the heir to the vineyard, they seized him and killed him. Let him who has ears hear."

The truth undermines our view of ourselves as independent and autonomous. Deep inside we know this house to be built on sand, that the walls of our castle of identity have no foundation, but we don't want to hear it. We want this illusion to be maintained. When the mirror of truth is held up to us, we feel fear, and the fear turns to anger. Wars result.

66

Jesus said, "Show me the stone which the builders have rejected. That one is the cornerstone."

Man is the builder. With the evolution of the opposing thumb, and his ability to conceive of that which does not yet exist, he became a tool maker par excellence. The more all-encompassing his created environment, the more believable the story—'I did this'. This belief in turn, has given rise to the concept of 'progress', and a better future—happiness postponed.

Those who do not subscribe to these beliefs represent a threat to the mainstream, because they have the ability to undermine this world view. Knowing, deep down, the shallow basis for these concepts, this in turn gives rise to fear, and then anger among the mainstream. Therefore they are rejected. Jesus says, 'These ones are the cornerstone,' because they will form the vanguard of his movement for change.

—— 67 ——

Jesus said, "If one who knows the all still feels a personal deficiency, he is completely deficient."

Sense of lack is one of the hallmarks of ego, the belief in a personal consciousness. We can have a deep intellectual understanding of Truth, but if we still feel separate, we have achieved nothing, for at the feeling level we still believe ourselves to be alone, at risk, and at the mercy of our fears and desires. Only when the investigation is complete at all levels—thought, feeling, and sense perception—are we free.

— 68 —

Jesus said, "Blessed are you when you are hated and persecuted. Wherever you have been persecuted they will find no place."

What Jesus is saying is, 'This world does not matter. It's not the ultimate reality. Whatever happens here, that takes you home, is a blessing'. Therefore if persecution in this world is what causes you to look inward for salvation, then good. Those who persecute you, are not looking there for happiness.

— 69 —

Jesus said, "Blessed are they who have been persecuted within themselves. It is they who have truly come to know the father. Blessed are the hungry, for the belly of him who desires will be filled."

To be persecuted within ourselves is to suffer internal destruction. Destruction of the ego, of beliefs, of conditioning. When this is gone, nothing obstructs the light, the love that we truly are.

Ramani Maharshi declared that the only thing which differentiated one truth seeker from another was their degree of ardour for the truth. Jesus also says, 'Blessed are the hungry (for truth)', for they shall receive the understanding they seek.

— 70 —

Jesus said, "That which you have will save you if you bring it forth from yourselves. That which you do not have within you will kill you if you do not have it within you."

Our desire for truth is that which we have to acknowledge and pay attention to. It may come in several forms—for example, a desire for an end to suffering, or a desire for peace. When 'brought forth' and given attention, this desire leads us to our true nature. Without the presence of this desire the illusory spell of human life, birth and death remains unchallenged and unbroken.

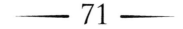

— 71 —

Jesus said, "I shall destroy this house, and no one will be able to build it [...]."

Our illusory world of separate existence, the house built on sand, is the one which Jesus intends to destroy. This is achieved through understanding our true nature. Anything truly understood cannot be forgotten—it is not possible to return to the state prior to understanding. This is why he says, "and no one will be able to build it".

— 72 —

A man said to him, "Tell my brothers to divide my father's possessions with me."

He said to him, "O man, who has made me a divider?"

He turned to his disciples and said to them, "I am not a divider, am I?"

Jesus shows his humourous side. He makes a joke. The man wants Jesus to resolve his worldly problem, to have his brothers deal with him fairly. When Jesus say 'I am not a divider, am I?", he is referring to the fact that his message is unity, oneness—in other words, 'There is only one, and you are that.'

—— 73 ——

Jesus said, "The harvest is great but the laborers are few. Beseech the Lord, therefore, to send out laborers to the harvest."

In this worldly realm, there are only a few who love truth and know their true nature, yet all seek salvation in the form of happiness. Jesus says, 'Pray, therefore for more guides to come, to show where this happiness can be found,' for most of us need a teacher to show us the way home.

— 74 —

He said, "O Lord, there are many around the drinking trough, but there is nothing in the cistern."

We intuitively know that peace, happiness, and an end to suffering are possible, but we look for them in objects, however, that is not where they are to be found. This worldly vessel, like the cistern, is empty. Once this fact has been completely absorbed, and we realise that the world will never quench our thirst for these things, we turn elsewhere in our investigation.

—— 75 ——

Jesus said, "Many are standing at the door, but it is the solitary who will enter the bridal chamber."

In the end, as human beings, we are alone. No one else can live our lives for us. We are each perfectly formed reflections of God, fully equipped for our own unique and intimate journey home. We depart when we're ready, and travel at our own pace.

76

Jesus said, "The kingdom of the father is like a merchant who had a consignment of merchandise and who discovered a pearl. That merchant was shrewd. He sold the merchandise and bought the pearl alone for himself. You too, seek his unfailing and enduring treasure where no moth comes near to devour and no worm destroys."

There is one essential difference between the treasure we seek, and everything else we have ever known. This treasure lasts forever, and contains within it everything else that ever existed. Once it is found, all else is redundant. This is why the merchant 'sold the merchandise and bought the pearl alone for himself'. Once he had found the pearl he needed nothing more.

Jesus said, "It is I who am the light which is above them all. It is I who am the all. From me did the all come forth, and unto me did the all extend. Split a piece of wood, and I am there. Lift up the stone, and you will find me there."

The encapsulation of Jesus entire teaching, of non-separation and unity. He says, "It is I who am the all"—including you, me, the entire universe and everything in it. In other words we are all one. We are not separate, rather we are all expressions of the one consciousness, also called God.

78

Jesus said, "Why have you come out into the desert? To see a reed shaken by the wind? And to see a man clothed in fine garments like your kings and your great men? Upon them are the fine garments, and they are unable to discern the truth."

The, 'reed shaken by the wind', expresses the very miracle of existence, of there being something rather than nothing—and when we hear the truth, something resonates within us and says, 'Yes! That's true!' We may not have the words to articulate it, but when we hear it, we recognise it. When this clarity is present, we are not deluded by the symbols of power of the world, by the 'men clothed in fine garments'.

79

A woman from the crowd said to him, "Blessed are the womb which bore you and the breasts which nourished you."

He said to her, "Blessed are those who have heard the word of the father and have truly kept it. For there will be days when you will say, 'Blessed are the womb which has not conceived and the breasts which have not given milk.'"

The only certainty in the world is change—this is why Jesus counsels against seeking blessings in the world. It is not possible to insulate oneself from age, accident, infirmity, wars—upheavals of all types. We can never know what will happen tomorrow. The only true 'Blessing' is to find that which does not change, that loving peace which is eternal— our true home. Therefore Jesus says, 'Blessed are those who have heard the word of the father and truly kept it'.

80

Jesus said, "He who has recognized the world has found the body, but he who has found the body is superior to the world."

To recognise the world is to know that manifestation, the physical universe, here called, 'the body' has no independent existence, no life of its own. It, and all life within it, are animated, for a time, by life itself. The one who understands this knows his true identity to be that which gives rise to that very animating life force.

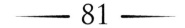

81

Jesus said, "Let him who has grown rich be king, and let him who possesses power renounce it."

'Let us create a world where those rich in understanding, and in humility, become our leaders, and those without such gifts relinquish whatever worldly power they have'.

—— 82 ——

Jesus said, "He who is near me is near the fire, and he who is far from me is far from the kingdom."

He who is near Jesus is near the fire of truth, which burns away our beliefs, fears and desires. When these are gone, only our true nature remains, that which we truly are, and we are at peace.

If the belief in a separate and personal consciousness remain, so do the fears and desires, and peace will forever elude us.

83

Jesus said, "The images are manifest to man, but the light in them remains concealed in the image of the light of the father. He will become manifest, but his image will remain concealed by his light."

Man sees the world, but not that which gives rise to the world. That which gives rise to the world is beingness itself, also called Brahman, which itself comes into existence out of the void, the potentiality of all things, also called Atman. Ultimately Brahman and Atman are one, and are not other than that which we also call God, or consciousness.

— 84 —

Jesus said, "When you see your likeness, you rejoice. But when you see your images which came into being before you, and which neither die nor become manifest, how much you will have to bear!"

When you see images of yourself you rejoice, because you think this is who you are. If however you were to envisage with the same clarity all the different memories of who you've been in this life, (the images which neither die nor become manifest) and the changes which your body-mind has undergone, how challenged would you be to reconcile the unchanging 'you' which you know yourself to be, and the constantly changing kaleidoscope of remembered images of 'you'.

— 85 —

Jesus said, "Adam came into being from a great power and a great wealth, but he did not become worthy of you. For had he been worthy, he would not have experienced death."

The disciples became worthy as a result of their opportunity to have lived with and learned from, Jesus. They experienced first hand what it is to live in truth. Such an opportunity is precious and rare in this world. For most of us who are interested in knowing our true nature, such a relationship is a most joyful and beautiful experience, and equally necessary.

86

Jesus said, "The foxes have their holes and the birds have their nests, but the son of man has no place to lay his head and rest."

Jesus is not of this world, and in truth, neither are we. There is no place of permanent rest for either of us here. We must look beyond the objective world to find true peace, and a 'place to lay our head and rest'.

87

Jesus said, "Wretched is the body that is dependent upon a body, and wretched is the soul that is dependent on these two."

To be afraid of death is to be afraid of life. 'Wretched therefore is the person who believes himself to be his body, for the threat of physical death is always close at hand. Wretched too is the one who identifies with his mind, for psychological fear is always there in the shadows, presaging the death of body-mind identification'.

— 88 —

Jesus said, "The angels and the prophets will come to you and give to you those things you (already) have. And you too, give them those things which you have, and say to yourselves, 'When will they come and take what is theirs?' "

You don't need anything more to be free. Everything required, you possess already. Not realising this however, you make worldly offerings, thinking this is all you can give, and ask the Lord, 'When will you rescue me?' In truth, happiness is available to you in every moment.

89

Jesus said, "Why do you wash the outside of the cup? Do you not realize that he who made the inside is the same one who made the outside?"

Many of us think that the external world, 'the outside of the cup' is all there is, and are therefore dedicated to maintaining and securing our existence within it, 'washing the cup', with knowledge, money, possessions, a fine self-image, and secure protections.

In reality, we never perceive the 'outside of the cup', we only ever perceive the 'inside'. We perceive thoughts, feelings, and sense perceptions, nothing more. In other words we don't actually perceive the world, rather we perceive our perceptions of it.

Therefore the 'outside' which we think is all that's real, is not perceived at all, and the 'inside' whose reality we consider tenuous, is in fact all that's perceived. Both the inside and the apparent outside of the cup, are God's creation.

— 90 —

Jesus said, "Come unto me, for my yoke is easy and my lordship is mild, and you will find repose for yourselves."

Many of us are prepared to pay a high price to pursue what seems like our personal destiny, our individuality, and our freedom. The price comes in the form of fears and desires—and the endless cycle of activity arising from our desire to achieve happiness, and keep death away. This we pursue, even though deep inside we know the struggle will inevitably end in failure.

For those who are prepared to surrender their apparent individuality, their belief in a personal consciousness, however, a remarkable discovery is made—we don't really give up anything at all. We find ourselves free of our fears and desires, in stillness, undiminished in any way, and we are at peace.

—— 91 ——

They said to him, "Tell us who you are so that we may believe in you."

He said to them, "You read the face of the sky and of the earth, but you have not recognized the one who is before you, and you do not know how to read this moment."

Conventional beliefs are taken to be facts, without the necessary supporting evidence. As such they are without substance or value, and preclude clear seeing. When we know something to be true it's because we recognise the truth in it, not because we have been told to believe it. It is as if we already knew it to be true but had simply obscured the fact.

Because they do not recognise the truth which Jesus speaks, they say, 'Tell us who you are', and ask for other reasons to believe in him, to quell their doubts.

When Jesus also says, '..and you do not know how to read this moment,' what he means is, 'you don't understand the significance of the 'now', of this very moment. Past and future are either remembered or imagined, but now is the only reality—it contains everything.

—— 92 ——

Jesus said, "Seek and you will find. Yet, what you asked me about in former times and which I did not tell you then, now I do desire to tell, but you do not inquire after it."

Lover's of truth have asked deep questions since time immemorial, and somehow, the universe finds a way to answer these questions. Over these many centuries, however, there have only been a small number of teachers with the stature of Jesus. When he speaks above, he does so as the Father, as God, who now desires to 'tell', through the manifestation of Jesus in the world.

93

\<Jesus said,\> "Do not give what is holy to dogs, lest they throw them on the dung-heap. Do not throw the pearls to swine, lest they [...] it [...]."

The truth is precious. The presence of an authentic teacher is precious. For this reason most of the highest teachings in all the major traditions have, in the past, been secret—given to an aspirant only when he or she was deemed able to truly absorb them. Today, everything is available to everyone. Nonetheless it is still the case that only those who are looking, will find the answers they seek. To foist truth upon those who are not looking, is pointless and ineffective, and fails to acknowledge our individual freedom to seek happiness on our own terms.

— 94 —

Jesus said, "He who seeks will find, and he who knocks will be let in."

Grace is always present, at all times and in all situations. Truly, we are never separate, alone. No matter how many times we turn away from the opportunity to surrender to truth, the invitation always remains open to return home, to find peace. God's grace is infinite.

—— 95 ——

Jesus said, "If you have money, do not lend it at interest, but give it to one from whom you will not get it back."

Oneness, not separation is Jesus' message. When we see others as separate, then we see ourselves as separate also, and in trying to protect ourselves and grow our material wealth, 'we lend money only for interest'. Similarly, to give it to one 'from whom we will not get it back', is a challenge if we see the other as separate, but is of no consequence if we see the other as us. Nothing is lost when we give what is ours to ourselves.

— 96 —

Jesus said, "The kingdom of the father is like a certain woman. She took a little leaven, concealed it in some dough, and made it into large loaves. Let him who has ears hear."

The 'leaven' is the seed of truth, the catalyst, the glimpse of our true nature, which, once alive in us, allows us to grow in understanding—its presence felt in all aspects of our being.

—— 97 ——

Jesus said, "The kingdom of the father is like a certain woman who was carrying a jar full of meal. While she was walking on the road, still some distance from home, the handle of the jar broke and the meal emptied out behind her on the road. She did not realize it; she had noticed no accident. When she reached her house, she set the jar down and found it empty."

The meal stands for the riches of the world. When we follow the path of truth, along the way our attachment to worldly things falls away without us even noticing. In the end we find ourselves empty of fears and desires, yet missing nothing.

— 98 —

Jesus said, "The kingdom of the father is like a certain man who wanted to kill a powerful man. In his own house he drew his sword and stuck it into the wall in order to find out whether his hand could carry through. Then he slew the powerful man."

The enemy we wish to slay is ignorance, our identity with ourselves as body-minds. The weapon is the sword of truth. We begin by being truthful with ourselves. Then we take that truth into the world, and live it.

99

The disciples said to him, "Your brothers and your mother are standing outside."

He said to them, "Those here who do the will of my father are my brothers and my mother. It is they who will enter the kingdom of my father."

When the veil of ignorance is lifted, when we are no longer identified with our body-minds, then we become transparent. Other like-minded lovers of truth are equally transparent to us and together we are one. This is love, and is the highest form of relationship, closer even than brother or mother. This is the kingdom of which Jesus speaks.

100

They showed Jesus a gold coin and said to him, "Caesar's men demand taxes from us."

He said to them, "Give Caesar what belongs to Caesar, give God what belongs to God, and give me what is mine."

Caesar represents the physical universe, God is that in which the physical universe has its existence, and Jesus stands for consciousness, life itself.

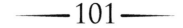

—— 101 ——

\<Jesus said,\> "Whoever does not hate his father and his mother as I do cannot become a disciple to me. And whoever does not love his father and his mother as I do cannot become a disciple to me. For my mother [...], but my true mother gave me life."

When Jesus says he hates his mother and father, it is the lie of his identity as their son, bound in a physical body, that he detests, together with all the societal structures that maintain that untruth. His real father and mother are those forces of love and life, which truly gave birth to him.

—102—

Jesus said, "Woe to the Pharisees, for they are like a dog sleeping in the manger of oxen, for neither does he eat nor does he let the oxen eat."

Truth is love. In the absence of love, truth is concealed. The Pharisees neither pursue truth themselves, nor permit others to do so. On the contrary, they seek to perpetuate ignorance. They remain with us today.

—103—

Jesus said, "Fortunate is the man who knows where the brigands will enter, so that he may get up, muster his domain, and arm himself before they invade."

'We must become wise, and undress ourselves'. Investigation gives rise to self-knowledge. We come to understand the domains of thought, feeling and sense-perception. In turn we come to know those subtle mentations that have the power to take us away from our true nature, 'where the brigands enter'. Armed with this knowledge we remain vigilant, until, through investigation, all doubts have been rendered powerless, and we find ourselves at peace.

—104—

They said to Jesus, "Come, let us pray today and let us fast."

Jesus said, "What is the sin that I have committed, or wherein have I been defeated? But when the bridegroom leaves the bridal chamber, then let them fast and pray."

On the journey we may engage in many practices to helps us remain steadfast, but when the battle is won, there is nothing more to be done. Then is the time for celebration. Jesus encourages them to celebrate with him, while he is in the world.

Jesus said, "He who knows the father and the mother will be called the son of a harlot."

To, 'know the father and the mother', is to claim identity as their son, that is, to give precedence to this apparent reality, and to deny one's true identity. Authentic investigation reveals the claim to be false.

—— 106 ——

Jesus said, "When you make the two one, you will become the sons of man, and when you say, 'Mountain, move away,' it will move away."

When the distinction between subject and object vanishes, we see that all is one. Me as you, you as me. All separation dissolves and this conscious loving presence, is all that remains. Then we are 'the sons of man', and the mountain to be moved, has no more substance than a thought.

Jesus said, "The kingdom is like a shepherd who had a hundred sheep. One of them, the largest, went astray. He left the ninety-nine sheep and looked for that one until he found it. When he had gone to such trouble, he said to the sheep, 'I care for you more than the ninety-nine.'"

Consciousness is not divisible. Its value is not in numbers. In truth I am more than my brother's keeper, I am my brother. When any of us are lost, I am lost. We seek the lost sheep, because we seek to be returned to our pristine state, as one.

—108—

Jesus said, "He who will drink from my mouth will become like me. I myself shall become he, and the things that are hidden will be revealed to him."

To 'drink from Jesus mouth', is to be open to his teaching, to listen to his words, and to allow them to be fully absorbed. This gives rise to understanding, which cannot be lost, and which transforms us, causing us to become like him. In this openness to the possibility of consciousness being universal, impersonal, the universe becomes magical, revealing to us our intimate interconnectedness with all things.

—— 109 ——

Jesus said, "The kingdom is like a man who had a hidden treasure in his field without knowing it. And after he died, he left it to his son. The son did not know (about the treasure). He inherited the field and sold it. And the one who bought it went plowing and found the treasure. He began to lend money at interest to whomever he wished."

Ignorance of our true nature, of the treasure hidden in plain sight, is ingrained in our societies, built into the very fabric of our cultures. Each generation, born in innocence, is unwittingly educated in untruth from birth. Yet through grace, some are shown reality. From them the truth shines out, touching all around them.

—— 110 ——

Jesus said, "Whoever finds the world and becomes rich, let him renounce the world."

To become rich is to have the opportunity to discover the empty promise of wealth. Having fully seen the futility of this enterprise, we look elsewhere for salvation, ultimately turning inward to investigate the true nature of our being.

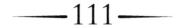

— 111 —

Jesus said, "The heavens and the earth will be rolled up in your presence. And the one who lives from the living one will not see death." Does not Jesus say, "Whoever finds himself is superior to the world?"

The universe, time and space exist only within the greater reality we call God, who is beyond time, and all other limitations. Since our true nature is not other than that, we too are timeless, knowing neither birth nor death.

—— 112 ——

Jesus said, "Woe to the flesh that depends on the soul; woe to the soul that depends on the flesh."

The body that identifies with mind, and the mind that identifies with body are both pursuing false beliefs, which do not lead to happiness. Instead let us look to what is real, to what our real identity is.

His disciples said to him, "When will the kingdom come?"

<Jesus said,> "It will not come by waiting for it. It will not be a matter of saying 'here it is' or 'there it is.' Rather, the kingdom of the father is spread out upon the earth, and men do not see it."

To wait for the kingdom, is to place it in the future, always out of reach. In this way we abdicate responsibility for being present to it now. By remaining in not-knowing, open to this possibility, then through Grace, we come to experience the kingdom, 'spread out upon the earth' in each and every moment.

—114—

Simon Peter said to him, "Let Mary leave us, for women are not worthy of life."

Jesus said, "I myself shall lead her in order to make her male, so that she too may become a living spirit resembling you males. For every woman who will make herself male will enter the kingdom of heaven."

Jesus finds a way to introduce equality in a male dominated society. In the realm of freedom and truth, Jesus creates a way whereby by following him, all are to be considered equal, both male and female, and all are to receive the same opportunity for happiness.

THE GOSPEL
ACCORDING TO THOMAS

Selection made from James M. Robinson, ed.,
The Nag Hammadi Library, revised edition.
HarperCollins, San Francisco, 1990.

Printed in Great Britain
by Amazon

42233892R00071